Wealth and Purpose:

HOW TO UNLOCK YOUR FINANCES AND SUCCESS WITH GOD'S KINGDOM PRINCIPLES

Dr. Latina C. Campbell

Print ISBN: 978-1-955312-93-6

eBook ISBN: 978-1-955312-94-3

Printed in the United States of America

Story Corner Publishing & Consulting, Inc.

Chesapeake, VA 23321

Storycornerpublishing@yahoo.com

www.StoryCornerPublishing.com

Dedicated

I dedicate this book to everyone who is tired of settling for less and knows they should have more in life, but do not know how to get it.

Heavenly Father,

Thank You for revealing Your heart for financial freedom and success. Help me to align my life with Your principles and to steward the blessings You've entrusted to me. May everything I do glorify You and bring others into Your Kingdom, in Yeshua's name, Amen.

"But remember the LORD your God, for it is he who gives you the ability to produce wealth, and so confirms his covenant, which he swore to your ancestors, as it is today." Deuteronomy 8:18

Contents

Introduction

EMBRACING KINGDOM WEALTH

God has a plan for every believer—a plan that includes prosperity, abundance, and success. Yet, many Believers of Christ struggle with the concept of wealth, associating it with greed or worldliness. This misunderstanding has left many of God's children living far below their potential, trapped in financial lack and spiritual discouragement. But the truth is that God's Word is filled with promises of provision, abundance, and blessings for those who walk according to His ways.

In this book, we'll redefine wealth from a Kingdom perspective. Kingdom wealth is not about hoarding material possessions or chasing after worldly riches. Instead, it's about walking in divine alignment with God's will, knowing who you are in Jesus Christ/ Yeshua, and using the resources He entrusts to you to fulfill your purpose and bless others. Financial freedom is not just a dream— it's a reality for those who dare to believe and act on God's promises.

Why Financial Freedom Matters in God's Kingdom

Financial freedom is not just about paying off debts or building savings; it's about breaking free from anything that keeps you from fulfilling your God-given purpose. When you're weighed down by financial burdens, it's difficult to focus on your calling. But when you align with God's principles, He empowers you to live without lack, to bless others generously, and to further His Kingdom.

God is the ultimate provider and owner of all things:

- *"The earth is the Lord's, and everything in it, the world, and all who live in it."* (Psalm 24:1, NIV)

When you trust Him as your source, you step into a life of abundance that isn't dictated by the economy, your job, or your circumstances.

Our Identity as Kingdom Heirs

As believers, we are not just servants of God; we are His children. That means we are heirs to everything He owns (Romans 8:17). When you embrace this royal identity, you stop living in a scarcity mindset. Instead, you begin to walk in confidence, knowing that your Father in Heaven delights in providing for you.

This book will help you understand:

1. **Who you are in Jesus Christ/ Yeshua**: You are not a victim of circumstances but a victor through Jesus.

2. **God's promises for your finances**: His Word is full of declarations about His desire to bless you.

3. **How to align with His principles**: Spiritual success begins with obedience and faithfulness.

What to Expect in This Journey

This book is not just about teaching biblical truths—it's about transformation. Each chapter will guide you through a combination of spiritual principles, practical strategies, and actionable steps that will help you:

- Deepen your relationship with God.

- Break free from poverty mindsets and financial bondage.

- Cultivate habits of stewardship and generosity.

- Unlock the blessings and power God has already given you.

You'll also find:

- **Scriptures** to meditate on, revealing God's heart for your success.

- **Prayers** to help you connect with Him on a deeper level.

- **Affirmations** to renew your mind and declare your victory.

- **Practical Tips** to manage money wisely and grow your resources.

Above all, this book is about more than just money—it's about discovering the abundant life Jesus promised in John 10:10: *"I have come that they may have life, and have it to the full."* Financial freedom is one part of that fullness, but it's rooted in a deeper relationship with God. As you learn to seek His Kingdom first, He will take care of everything else (Matthew 6:33).

Through this journey, you'll come to understand that God's blessings are not limited. He has an unlimited supply, and He wants to use you as a vessel to bring His love, hope, and provision to the world. Are you ready to unlock the door to financial freedom and success with God?

Let's begin this Kingdom journey together.

Chapter 1

Understanding God's Plan for Prosperity

What is Kingdom Wealth?

Kingdom wealth is vastly different from the wealth the world chases. While worldly riches often lead to pride, selfish ambition, and discontentment, Kingdom wealth reflects God's nature—abundant, generous, and always for a higher purpose. It is wealth that flows through you, not just to you.

God's plan for prosperity is rooted in His love for us and His desire for us to live fulfilling, impactful lives. His definition of wealth encompasses more than money—it includes spiritual, emotional, relational, and material abundance. When we walk in His ways, we experience a holistic prosperity that allows us to thrive and bring glory to Him.

Key Scripture:

"The blessing of the Lord makes one rich, and He adds no sorrow with it." (Proverbs 10:22, NKJV)

This verse reminds us that God's blessings come without regret or guilt. They are designed to enrich our lives and enable us to bless others.

God's Covenant of Prosperity

From the beginning, God established a covenant with His people to bless them abundantly. This covenant was first seen with Abraham:

"I will make you into a great nation, and I will bless you; I will make your name great, and you will be a blessing." (Genesis 12:2, NIV)

Abraham's blessings were not only for him but for the nations through him. As believers in Christ, we are heirs of that same covenant (Galatians 3:29). This means God's promises of provision and success extend to us today.

- **Provision for His Purpose**: God's blessings are always tied to His purpose. He blesses us so we can fulfill our assignments and expand His Kingdom.

- **Prosperity as a Sign of His Favor**: While prosperity is not the ultimate measure of God's favor, it is often a byproduct of obedience and alignment with His will.

Common Misconceptions About Wealth in the Kingdom

1. "Money is the root of all evil."

Many misquote 1 Timothy 6:10, which actually says, *"For the love of money is a root of all kinds of evil."* Money itself is not evil—it is a tool. The problem arises when we idolize it or prioritize it over God.

2. "People of God should be poor to be holy."

Jesus/ Yeshua lived a life of purpose and provision. He was not impoverished; He had access to everything He needed to fulfill His mission. God desires for His children to thrive, not suffer in lack.

3. "God doesn't care about my finances."

On the contrary, God deeply cares about every aspect of your life, including your finances. He desires to bless you so you can live a testimony of His goodness.

Stewardship: A Key to Prosperity

Key Scripture:

"Moreover, it is required in stewards that one be found faithful." (1 Corinthians 4:2, NKJV)

God entrusts us with resources to manage wisely. When we are faithful stewards, we honor Him and position ourselves to receive more of His blessings. Stewardship involves:

1. **Recognizing God as the Source:** Everything we have comes from Him (Psalm 24:1).

2. **Managing Resources Wisely:** Planning, budgeting, and using resources responsibly.

3. **Being Generous:** Blessing others with what God has given us (2 Corinthians 9:6-8).

How to Align with God's Plan for Prosperity

1. **Seek God First:**

"But seek first His kingdom and His righteousness, and all these things will be given to you as well." (Matthew 6:33, NIV)

Prioritize God's will in your life, and He will meet all your needs.

2. **Meditate on His Promises:**

Reflect on scriptures that reveal God's heart for your prosperity, such as:

- *"The Lord will open the heavens, the storehouse of His bounty, to send rain on your land in season and to bless all the work of your hands."* (Deuteronomy 28:12, NIV)

- *"Beloved, I pray that you may prosper in all things and be in health, just as your soul prospers."* (3 John 1:2, NKJV)

3. **Obey His Principles:**

Obedience opens the door to God's blessings. Follow biblical principles such as tithing, generosity, and living with integrity.

Practical Reflection: Are You Ready to Prosper?

- Take an inventory of your beliefs about money. Do they align with God's Word, or are they shaped by fear or worldly views?

- Ask yourself how you are currently stewarding the resources God has given you. Are there areas where you can improve?

Prayer of Alignment

Father, I thank You for Your plan to prosper me and not harm me. Teach me to align my heart and actions with Your Word. Help me to be a faithful steward of the blessings You've entrusted to me, and use me to glorify Your name. I trust You as my source and provider. Amen.

Affirmations:

- *I am an heir of God's covenant of abundance.*

- *God is my source, and I trust Him to meet all my needs.*

- *I am a faithful steward of the resources God has entrusted to me.*

By understanding God's plan for prosperity, you can step into a life of abundance and purpose. This chapter lays the foundation for the journey ahead, helping you align your mind, heart, and actions with the truth of God's Word.

Chapter 2

REPENTANCE—THE FIRST STEP
TO BREAKTHROUGH

The Power of Repentance in Financial Freedom

Repentance is a divine reset button. It's the process by which we turn away from sin and align ourselves with God's will. Financial struggles are often rooted in spiritual issues such as poor stewardship, greed, fear, or a lack of trust in God. Without repentance, these spiritual blockages can keep us from experiencing the fullness of God's blessings.

Repentance is not merely about saying "I'm sorry"; it's about changing our minds, hearts, and actions to align with God's principles. True repentance brings renewal and positions us for breakthrough.

Key Scripture:

"Repent, then, and turn to God, so that your sins may be wiped out, that times of refreshing may come from the Lord." (Acts 3:19, NIV)

Through repentance, we allow God to wipe the slate clean, refresh our spirits, and restore us to His original plan of abundance and purpose.

Identifying Areas That Require Repentance

To experience financial freedom, it's important to examine areas where you may have fallen short of God's principles. This could include:

1. **Poor Stewardship:** Misusing resources, failing to budget, or living beyond your means.

2. **Lack of Generosity:** Neglecting to tithe or give to others as God leads.

3. **Fear or Doubt:** Trusting in money or worldly systems instead of God as your provider.

4. **Covetousness or Greed:** Desiring what others have or hoarding out of insecurity.

Reflection:

Ask the Holy Spirit to reveal areas where your mindset or actions regarding money are not in alignment with God's Word.

Breaking Free from the Spirit of Poverty

The spirit of poverty is a mindset that says, "I'll never have enough," "I'm not worthy of wealth," or "Riches are evil." This belief system keeps people trapped in lack, regardless of how much money they have.

Key Scripture:

"For God has not given us a spirit of fear, but of power and of love and of a sound mind." (2 Timothy 1:7, NKJV)

To break free:

1. **Acknowledge the Lies:** Recognize and reject thoughts and patterns that contradict God's promises of provision.

2. **Replace Them with Truth:** Declare God's Word over your finances (e.g., Philippians 4:19).

3. **Repent for Agreement:** If you've believed or acted in ways that align with poverty, ask God for forgiveness and choose to embrace His truth.

Steps to True Repentance

1. **Confession:**

Admit your sins and shortcomings to God. Be specific. For example:

- *"Lord, I confess that I have not trusted You with my finances."*

- *"I repent for overspending and neglecting to tithe."*

2. **Ask for Forgiveness:**

God is faithful to forgive when we approach Him with a sincere heart.

Key Scripture: *"If we confess our sins, He is faithful and just to forgive us our sins and to purify us from all unrighteousness."* (1 John 1:9, NIV)

3. **Turn Away from Sin:**

True repentance involves change. Commit to a new way of living that aligns with God's Word.

4. **Invite the Holy Spirit:**

Ask the Holy Spirit to guide you in making wise decisions and overcoming old habits.

Repentance Prayer

Heavenly Father, I come before You with a repentant heart. I confess that I have not always honored You with my finances or trusted You as my provider. Forgive me for mismanaging the blessings You have given me, for doubting Your provision, and for being led by fear or greed. Cleanse me from all unrighteousness and renew my mind. Help me to walk in alignment with Your principles and to steward my resources faithfully. In Jesus' name, Amen.

God's Response to Repentance

Repentance opens the door to God's mercy and grace. He is not a God of condemnation but a God of restoration. When we turn back to Him, He not only forgives us but also restores what was lost.

Key Scripture:

"I will restore to you the years that the swarming locust has eaten." (Joel 2:25, ESV)

When we repent, God begins to redeem the time, opportunities, and blessings we may have missed due to disobedience or ignorance.

Replacing Old Patterns with Kingdom Habits

After repentance, it's crucial to develop new habits that reflect your transformed mindset:

1. **Tithing Faithfully:** Honor God with the first fruits of your income (Malachi 3:10).

2. **Practicing Generosity:** Look for opportunities to bless others.

3. **Budgeting and Planning:** Manage your finances wisely as an act of worship.

4. **Daily Declarations:** Speak life over your finances. For example:

   - *"I am forgiven, redeemed, and restored."*

   - *"God is my source, and I trust Him to provide."*

Affirmations of Freedom

- *I am free from the spirit of poverty.*

- *I trust God as my provider and source of all abundance.*

- *I walk in alignment with God's principles, and I am positioned for breakthrough.*

Reflection Questions

- Are there specific financial habits or mindsets you need to repent of?

- How can you invite God into your financial decisions moving forward?

- What steps will you take to ensure your actions align with Kingdom principles?

Repentance is not just the starting point for financial freedom; it's the foundation for a life of abundance in God. By turning away from old patterns and aligning with God's ways, you position yourself to walk in His blessings and fulfill your Kingdom purpose.

Chapter 3
DISCOVERING YOUR ROYAL IDENTITY IN CHRIST

Our Identity as Kingdom Heirs

One of the greatest revelations a believer can have is understanding who they are in Christ. As children of God, we are more than mere servants—we are royalty, heirs to the Kingdom of Heaven, and ambassadors of God's authority on Earth. This identity comes with rights, responsibilities, and access to divine resources.

Key Scripture:

"But you are a chosen generation, a royal priesthood, a holy nation, His own special people, that you may proclaim the praises of Him who called you out of darkness into His marvelous light." (1 Peter 2:9, NKJV)

God has called us out of spiritual poverty into a life of abundance, not only in material things but also in spiritual riches, wisdom, and authority. To experience financial freedom and success, we must first embrace our royal identity.

What It Means to Be Royalty in Christ

1. **You Are a Child of the King:**

As a child of God, you are an heir to His Kingdom and all the resources of Heaven.

- *"The Spirit Himself bears witness with our spirit that we are children of God, and if children, then heirs—heirs of God and joint heirs with Christ."* (Romans 8:16-17, NKJV)

2. 2. You Have Authority:

Jesus has given believers authority over the enemy and the power to declare His will on Earth. This authority extends to every area of life, including finances.

- *"Behold, I give you the authority to trample on serpents and scorpions, and over all the power of the enemy, and nothing shall by any means hurt you."* (Luke 10:19, NKJV)

3. You Are Blessed to Be a Blessing:

Royalty comes with responsibility. God blesses us so that we can bless others and advance His Kingdom.

- *"And God is able to bless you abundantly, so that in all things at all times, having all that you need, you will abound in every good work."* (2 Corinthians 9:8, NIV)

Breaking Free from the Orphan Spirit

Many Believers of Christ live with an "orphan spirit," a mindset of lack and rejection, even though they are sons and daughters of the King. This spirit manifests in fear, insecurity, and a constant striving for approval. To embrace your royal identity, you must renounce the orphan spirit and accept God's unconditional love.

Key Scripture:

"The Spirit you received does not make you slaves, so that you live in fear again; rather, the Spirit you received brought about your adoption to sonship. And by Him we cry, 'Abba, Father.'" (Romans 8:15, NIV)

Steps to Break Free:

1. **Acknowledge God as Your Father:** Rest in His love and trust in His provision.

2. **Renounce Lies of Lack and Rejection:** Replace them with the truth of God's promises.

3. **Speak Your Identity:** Declare who you are in Christ daily.

Understanding Your Heavenly Inheritance

As heirs of God, we have access to His unlimited resources. However, this inheritance is not automatic; it requires faith and alignment with God's principles to activate.

Key Scripture:

"His divine power has given us everything we need for a godly life through our knowledge of Him who called us by His own glory and goodness." (2 Peter 1:3, NIV)

1. **Spiritual Riches:** Wisdom, peace, joy, and the fruit of the Spirit.

2. **Material Provision:** God supplies all your needs according to His riches in glory (Philippians 4:19).

3. **Kingdom Authority:** Power to declare God's will, bind the enemy, and walk in victory.

Practical Steps to Embrace Your Royal Identity

1. Meditate on God's Word:

Study scriptures that reveal your identity in Yeshua, such as:

- Ephesians 2:10: *"For we are God's masterpiece."*

- Jeremiah 29:11: *"For I know the plans I have for you, declares the Lord."*

2. Renew Your Mind:

Replace old mindsets of unworthiness or lack with Kingdom truths.

- **Affirmation:** *"I am a child of God, a co-heir with Christ, and I walk in His authority and abundance."*

3. Live with Confidence and Purpose:

Make decisions based on your royal identity, not fear or insecurity.

4. Align with Kingdom Principles:

Act in obedience to God's Word regarding stewardship, generosity, and faith.

Prayer of Royal Identity

Father, I thank You for calling me Your child and making me an heir of Your Kingdom. I renounce the orphan spirit and every lie that has kept me in lack or fear. Help me to walk in the authority, abundance, and purpose You have given me. Renew my mind, Lord, and teach me to live as royalty in Your Kingdom. In Jesus' name, Amen.

Walking in Kingdom Wealth

Understanding your royal identity is the key to walking in Kingdom wealth. When you know who you are in Christ, you stop striving and start trusting. You live from a place of abundance, knowing that your Father in Heaven is your provider and source.

Key Scripture:

"Now to Him who is able to do exceedingly abundantly above all that we ask or think, according to the power that works in us." (Ephesians 3:20, NKJV)

Reflection Questions

- Do you truly see yourself as a child of God and an heir to His Kingdom?

- Are there any lies or limiting beliefs about your identity that you need to renounce?

- How can you walk in greater confidence and authority as a Kingdom heir?

Affirmations of Royalty

- *I am a child of the King, and I live in His abundance.*

- *I have been adopted into God's family and walk in His authority.*

- *I am blessed to be a blessing to others.*

This chapter invites you to embrace your royal identity and step into the fullness of what God has for you. When you know who you are in Christ, you gain the confidence to claim your inheritance and live a life of purpose, abundance, and victory.

Introductory Questions

- Is your garden or landscape a high-risk island or ...

- Are there any known introduced pests? Check to identify that you know your ...

- ... know ... where ... garden ...

Chapter 4

ACTIVATING THE POWER OF GOD IN YOUR LIFE

The Authority of a Believer

As followers of Jesus, we are not powerless in this world. God has given us His Spirit, His Word, and His authority to live victoriously and fulfill His purposes. Activating this power is essential for financial freedom and success because it shifts us from relying on our own abilities to operating in God's limitless resources and wisdom.

Key Scripture:

"Behold, I give you the authority to trample on serpents and scorpions, and over all the power of the enemy, and nothing shall by any means hurt you." (Luke 10:19, NKJV)

The power of God in your life is not passive; it must be activated through faith, obedience, and alignment with His Word. This chapter will explore practical ways to connect with God on a deeper level and walk in the authority He has given you.

What is God's Power?

God's power is His ability to do exceedingly above all we can ask or imagine (Ephesians 3:20). It includes:

1. **Spiritual Power:** The ability to resist temptation, overcome spiritual battles, and walk in holiness.

2. **Creative Power:** Wisdom and inspiration to create solutions, build wealth, and fulfill your God-given purpose.

3. **Resurrection Power:** The same power that raised Christ from the dead lives in us, enabling us to overcome challenges and experience victory.

- *"And if the Spirit of Him who raised Yeshua from the dead is living in you, He who raised Christ from the dead will also give life to your mortal bodies because of His Spirit who lives in you."* (Romans 8:11, NIV)

How to Activate God's Power

1. Deepen Your Relationship with God

The power of God flows through intimacy with Him. The more you know Him, the more you can operate in His authority.

Practical Steps:

- **Spend Time in Prayer:** Prayer is your lifeline to God. Through consistent communication, you align with His will and receive His strength.

- **Worship:** Worship shifts your focus from your limitations to God's greatness, opening the door for His power to work in your life.

- **Study the Word:** God's power is revealed in His Word. By meditating on Scripture, you strengthen your faith and equip yourself with spiritual tools.

2. Walk by Faith, Not by Sight

Faith is the key to unlocking the supernatural. Without it, we cannot fully access God's promises.

- *"And without faith, it is impossible to please God, because anyone who comes to Him must believe that He exists and that He rewards those who earnestly seek Him."* (Hebrews 11:6, NIV)

Faith in Action:

- Speak life over your situation. Use affirmations grounded in Scripture to declare God's promises.

- Step out in obedience, even when the path isn't clear. Faith often requires action before the manifestation of results.

3. Use the Authority of Yeshua's Name

The name of Yeshua carries power and authority over every situation, including finances, health, and relationships.

- *"And whatever you ask in My name, that I will do, that the Father may be glorified in the Son."* (John 14:13, NKJV)

Practical Application:

- Pray boldly in the name of Jesus/ Yeshua, knowing that His authority backs your requests.

- Rebuke spiritual attacks and declare victory using the name of Jesus.

4. Invite the Holy Spirit

The Holy Spirit is the source of God's power in your life. He guides, comforts, and empowers you to live out God's purpose.

- *"But you will receive power when the Holy Spirit comes on you; and you will be My witnesses in Jerusalem, and in all Judea and Samaria, and to the ends of the earth."* (Acts 1:8, NIV)

Practical Steps:

- Ask the Holy Spirit to fill you daily.

- Listen for His guidance in decision-making, especially in financial matters.

- Yield to His leading, even when it challenges your comfort zone.

Overcoming Spiritual Hindrances

Sometimes, spiritual barriers can block the flow of God's power in our lives. These hindrances include:

1. **Unbelief:** Doubting God's promises limits His power.

   - *"He did not do many miracles there because of their lack of faith."* (Matthew 13:58, NIV)

2. **Sin and Disobedience:** Sin separates us from God and weakens our connection to His power.

   - *"If I had cherished sin in my heart, the Lord would not have listened."* (Psalm 66:18, NIV)

3. **Fear:** Fear paralyzes faith and keeps us from stepping into God's promises.

   - *"For God has not given us a spirit of fear, but of power and of love and of a sound mind."* (2 Timothy 1:7, NKJV)

How to Overcome:

- Confess and repent of any known sin.

- Meditate on God's promises to build faith.

- Speak against fear and declare God's power over your life.

Prayers for Activation

1. Prayer for God's Power:

Heavenly Father, I thank You for the power You have given me through Your Spirit. Help me to walk in faith and operate in the authority of Yeshua's name. Fill me with Your Holy Spirit and let Your power flow through me in every area of my life. In Yeshua's name, Amen.

2. Prayer Against Hindrances:

Lord, I renounce all doubt, fear, and sin that has hindered Your power in my life. I surrender completely to You and ask for a fresh outpouring of Your Spirit. Strengthen me to walk in obedience and boldness. In Yeshua's name, Amen.

Affirmations of Power

- *I am filled with the power of the Holy Spirit and walk in authority.*

- *I overcome every challenge by the power of God at work in me.*

- *The name of Jesus gives me victory over every situation.*

Reflection Questions

- Are you actively deepening your relationship with God to access His power?

- What areas of your life require faith and bold action?

- Are there any spiritual hindrances you need to address to fully activate God's power?

Living a Life of Power and Purpose

When you activate the power of God in your life, you step into a realm of limitless possibilities. Financial success and freedom are not achieved through human effort alone but by tapping into the divine power that God has placed within you. Trust in His promises, walk in His authority, and allow His Spirit to guide you into a life of abundance and purpose.

Key Scripture:

"For the kingdom of God is not a matter of talk but of power." (1 Corinthians 4:20, NIV)

Chapter 5

SPIRITUAL PRINCIPLES OF FINANCIAL SUCCESS

God's Blueprint for Financial Prosperity

Financial success in God's Kingdom is built on spiritual principles that align with His Word. These principles go beyond mere financial strategies; they are rooted in obedience, faith, stewardship, and generosity. When applied consistently, these principles unlock divine provision and establish a foundation for lasting abundance.

Key Scripture:

"But seek first the Kingdom of God and His righteousness, and all these things will be added to you." (Matthew 6:33, ESV)

True financial success begins with prioritizing God's Kingdom. When you align your finances with His will, you create a life that reflects His provision, purpose, and power.

Principle 1: God Owns Everything

The first step to financial success is recognizing that God is the ultimate owner of all things. As His children, we are stewards of His resources.

Key Scripture:

"The earth is the Lord's, and everything in it, the world, and all who live in it." (Psalm 24:1, NIV)

Implication:

- You are not the owner of your money, time, or talents; you are a manager.

- Every financial decision should reflect God's will and purpose.

Action Steps:

1. Acknowledge God's ownership of your resources through prayer.

2. Seek His guidance before making financial decisions.

3. Regularly dedicate your finances to His Kingdom.

Principle 2: Tithing and Generosity

Tithing is a biblical act of faith and obedience, while generosity reflects the heart of God. Both are essential for financial success in the Kingdom.

Key Scriptures:

- *"Bring the whole tithe into the storehouse, that there may be food in My house. Test Me in this," says the Lord Almighty, "and see if I will not throw open the floodgates of heaven and pour out so much blessing that there will not be room enough to store it."* (Malachi 3:10, NIV)

- *"Give, and it will be given to you. A good measure, pressed down, shaken together and running over, will be poured into your lap. For with the measure you use, it will be measured to you."* (Luke 6:38, NIV)

Benefits of Tithing and Giving:

1. Opens the door to God's supernatural provision.

2. Breaks the hold of greed and materialism.

3. Aligns your heart with God's purposes.

Action Steps:

- Commit to tithing 10% of your income to your local church.

- Practice generosity by giving to others in need, missions, or Kingdom-building initiatives.

Principle 3: Faithful Stewardship

Stewardship is the responsible management of the resources God has entrusted to you. Financial success requires wisdom, discipline, and accountability.

Key Scripture:

"Moreover, it is required in stewards that one be found faithful." (1 Corinthians 4:2, NKJV)

Characteristics of a Faithful Steward:

1. **Budgeting:** Create a plan for your finances that reflects your priorities.

2. **Saving:** Prepare for the future while trusting God for provision.

3. **Avoiding Debt:** Live within your means and seek to eliminate unnecessary debt.

Action Steps:

- Create a monthly budget that aligns with your income and expenses.

- Set aside a portion of your income for savings and emergencies.

- Pray for wisdom before making major financial commitments.

Principle 4: Diligence and Hard Work

God blesses diligence and hard work. Laziness and procrastination can hinder financial progress, while a strong work ethic honors God and opens doors for opportunities.

Key Scripture:

"The plans of the diligent lead surely to abundance, but everyone who is hasty comes only to poverty." (Proverbs 21:5, ESV)

Implication:

- Success requires effort and perseverance.
- While we rely on God, we also take practical steps to achieve our goals.

Action Steps:

- Set clear financial goals and work consistently toward them.
- Seek to improve your skills and maximize your earning potential.
- Avoid get-rich-quick schemes; focus on steady, honest growth.

Principle 5: Speaking Life Over Your Finances

Words have creative power. When you speak in alignment with God's Word, you release His blessings into your life. Conversely, negative or fearful speech can hinder financial success.

Key Scripture:

"Death and life are in the power of the tongue, and those who love it will eat its fruit." (Proverbs 18:21, NKJV)

Practical Application:

- Replace complaints or worries about money with declarations of God's promises.

- Speak affirmations daily, such as:

- *"God supplies all my needs according to His riches in glory."* (Philippians 4:19)

- *"I am the head and not the tail, above and not beneath."* (Deuteronomy 28:13)

Principle 6: Trusting God as Your Provider

Financial success requires trusting God as your ultimate source. Jobs, investments, and other resources are channels, but God is the source of all provision.

Key Scripture:

"And my God will meet all your needs according to the riches of His glory in Christ Jesus." (Philippians 4:19, NIV)

Implication:

- Trust eliminates fear and worry about finances.

- Trust allows you to act in faith, even when resources seem scarce.

Action Steps:

- Practice gratitude for what you have, trusting God for more.

- Refrain from hoarding or fearing lack; give generously and trust God to replenish.

Principle 7: Kingdom Purpose for Wealth

Financial success in God's Kingdom is never self-centered. Wealth is a tool to fulfill God's purposes, bless others, and advance His Kingdom.

Key Scripture:

"You will be made rich in every way so that you can be generous on every occasion, and through us your generosity will result in thanksgiving to God." (2 Corinthians 9:11, NIV)

Action Steps:

1. Align your financial goals with God's purposes (e.g., supporting ministries, helping the needy, funding Kingdom projects).

2. Ask God to reveal how He wants you to use the resources He entrusts to you.

Prayers for Financial Success

1. Prayer for Stewardship:

Heavenly Father, I acknowledge that everything I have belongs to You. Help me to steward Your resources wisely and to honor You in all my financial decisions. Teach me to budget, save, and give in a way that reflects Your Kingdom. In Jesus' name, Amen.

2. Prayer for Generosity:

Lord, create in me a generous heart. Let me be a cheerful giver who reflects Your love and provision. Use my finances to advance Your Kingdom and bless others. In Jesus' name, Amen.

Affirmations of Financial Success

- *I am a faithful steward of God's resources.*

- *I am blessed to be a blessing.*

- *God supplies all my needs and gives me the power to create wealth.*

Reflection Questions

1. Are there areas in your financial life where you need to grow in stewardship or faith?

2. How can you align your finances more closely with God's principles?

3. Are you trusting God fully as your provider, or are you relying on your own strength?

Living in Financial Freedom and Success

When you apply these spiritual principles, you shift your financial foundation from worldly systems to God's unshakable Kingdom. Success is no longer defined by how much you accumulate but by how faithfully you manage and multiply what God entrusts to you. By living according to His principles, you position yourself to experience His blessings, fulfill your purpose, and impact others for His glory.

Key Scripture:

"Honor the Lord with your wealth and with the firstfruits of all your produce; then your barns will be filled with plenty, and your vats will be bursting with wine." (Proverbs 3:9-10, ESV)

Chapter 6

PRACTICAL STEPS TO FINANCIAL FREEDOM

Walking Out God's Plan for Financial Freedom

Financial freedom is a goal that many desire but few achieve because it requires discipline, faith, and action. While spiritual principles lay the foundation, practical steps build the framework for a life free from financial bondage. These steps blend biblical wisdom with actionable strategies to help you live debt-free, grow wealth, and steward your finances wisely.

Key Scripture:

"The plans of the diligent lead surely to abundance, but everyone who is hasty comes only to poverty." (Proverbs 21:5, ESV)

Financial freedom starts with a plan, progresses with diligent action, and thrives under God's guidance. This chapter outlines the practical steps to transform your financial situation and live in the freedom God desires for you.

Step 1: Establish a Vision for Your Finances

Scripture:

"Where there is no vision, the people perish." (Proverbs 29:18, KJV)

Financial freedom begins with clarity. Define what financial freedom looks like for you. This vision should align with your personal goals and God's purpose for your life.

Action Steps:

1. **Pray for Direction:** Seek God's guidance to align your financial goals with His will.

2. **Set Specific Goals:** Write down short-term (e.g., paying off debt), medium-term (e.g., saving for a home), and long-term goals (e.g., retirement or funding a ministry).

3. **Visualize Success:** Create a financial vision board to keep you focused and motivated.

Step 2: Create a Budget

Scripture:

"Be sure you know the condition of your flocks, give careful attention to your herds." (Proverbs 27:23, NIV)

A budget is a financial plan that helps you allocate your income wisely. It is a critical tool for managing money and avoiding unnecessary spending.

Action Steps:

1. **Track Income and Expenses:** Write down all sources of income and every expense for at least one month.

2. **Prioritize Needs Over Wants:** Allocate funds for necessities (e.g., housing, food, and transportation) before discretionary spending.

3. **Use Tools and Apps:** Use budgeting tools like spreadsheets, apps, or software to simplify the process.

4. **Adjust Regularly:** Review and revise your budget monthly to reflect changes in income or expenses.

Step 3: Eliminate Debt

Scripture:

"The rich rule over the poor, and the borrower is slave to the lender." (Proverbs 22:7, NIV)

Debt is one of the greatest barriers to financial freedom. By tackling debt strategically, you can free up resources to save, invest, and give generously.

Action Steps:

1. **List Your Debts:** Write down all debts, including balances, interest rates, and minimum payments.

2. **Choose a Debt Payoff Method:**

   - *Snowball Method:* Pay off the smallest debt first, then roll that payment into the next debt.

   - *Avalanche Method:* Pay off the debt with the highest interest rate first to save money over time.

3. **Avoid New Debt:** Commit to living within your means and refrain from using credit cards unless you can pay the balance in full each month.

4. **Pray for Breakthrough:** Ask God for wisdom, discipline, and supernatural provision to overcome debt.

Step 4: Build an Emergency Fund

Scripture:

"Go to the ant, you sluggard; consider its ways and be wise! It stores its provisions in summer and gathers its food at harvest." (Proverbs 6:6-8, NIV)

An emergency fund acts as a financial buffer for unexpected expenses, such as medical bills, car repairs, or job loss.

Action Steps:

1. **Start Small:** Save $1,000 as an initial emergency fund.

2. **Aim for 3-6 Months of Expenses:** Gradually increase your savings to cover three to six months of living expenses.

3. **Automate Savings:** Set up automatic transfers to a separate savings account to build your fund consistently.

Step 5: Save and Invest Wisely

Scripture:

"Dishonest money dwindles away, but whoever gathers money little by little makes it grow." (Proverbs 13:11, NIV)

Saving and investing are essential for building wealth and achieving financial freedom. While saving provides security, investing allows your money to grow over time.

Action Steps:

1. **Set Savings Goals:** Save for specific purposes, such as a home, education, or retirement.

2. **Learn About Investing:** Educate yourself on investment options like stocks, bonds, mutual funds, and real estate.

3. **Seek Advice:** Consult with a financial advisor or trusted mentor to create an investment strategy.

4. **Invest Consistently:** Start small and contribute regularly to your investments, even during uncertain times.

Step 6: Practice Generosity

Scripture:

"Give, and it will be given to you. A good measure, pressed down, shaken together and running over, will be poured into your lap." (Luke 6:38, NIV)

Generosity is a Kingdom principle that opens the door for God's blessings. Giving not only impacts others but also cultivates a heart of gratitude and trust in God.

Action Steps:

1. **Tithe Faithfully:** Give 10% of your income to your local church as an act of worship and obedience.

2. **Give Beyond the Tithe:** Support charities, missions, or individuals in need.

3. **Be a Cheerful Giver:** Give with joy, trusting that God will provide for your needs.

Step 7: Develop Financial Literacy

Scripture:

"By wisdom a house is built, and through understanding it is established." (Proverbs 24:3, NIV)

Financial literacy is the foundation for making wise decisions about money. By increasing your knowledge, you equip yourself to manage wealth effectively.

Action Steps:

1. **Read Books and Articles:** Study financial topics from a biblical perspective.

2. **Take Courses:** Enroll in classes or workshops on budgeting, investing, or entrepreneurship.

3. **Learn from Experts:** Seek guidance from financial mentors or professionals.

Step 8: Develop Multiple Streams of Income

Scripture:

"Invest in seven ventures, yes, in eight; you do not know what disaster may come upon the land." (Ecclesiastes 11:2, NIV)

Relying on a single source of income can be risky. Diversifying your income streams provides stability and increases your ability to build wealth.

Action Steps:

1. **Identify Your Skills:** Use your talents and passions to create additional income sources.

2. **Start a Side Hustle:** Explore freelance work, consulting, or online businesses.

3. **Invest in Passive Income:** Consider real estate, dividend-paying stocks, or royalties.

Prayers for Financial Freedom

1. Prayer for Wisdom:

Lord, grant me wisdom to manage my finances according to Your will. Help me make wise decisions and honor You with my resources. In Jesus' name, Amen.

2. Prayer for Debt Freedom:

Heavenly Father, I ask for Your strength and provision to overcome my debts. Guide me to be disciplined and faithful as I work toward financial freedom. In Jesus' name, Amen.

3. Prayer for Generosity:

Lord, create in me a generous heart. Teach me to trust You with my finances and to give cheerfully to advance Your Kingdom. In Jesus' name, Amen.

Affirmations for Financial Freedom

- *I am disciplined and faithful in managing my finances.*

- *God supplies all my needs, and I live in abundance.*

- *I am debt-free and a wise steward of God's resources.*

Reflection Questions

1. Are you taking practical steps to align your finances with God's principles?

2. What changes can you make to improve your budgeting, saving, or giving habits?

3. How can you use your resources to honor God and bless others?

The Journey to Freedom

Financial freedom is not an overnight process but a journey of faith, discipline, and obedience. By applying these practical steps, you position yourself to live debt-free, grow wealth, and experience the joy of generosity. With God as your guide, financial freedom is not only possible—it is part of His abundant plan for your life.

Key Scripture:

"The blessing of the Lord brings wealth, without painful toil for it." (Proverbs 10:22, NIV)

Chapter 7

Connecting with God on a Deeper Level

The Foundation of a Deep Relationship with God

True financial freedom and success are rooted in a vibrant, intimate relationship with God. Connecting with Him on a deeper level allows you to hear His voice, align your life with His will, and access His wisdom and power. God desires a personal relationship with you that transforms every area of your life, including your finances.

Key Scripture:

"Draw near to God, and He will draw near to you." (James 4:8, ESV)

This chapter explores practical and spiritual ways to deepen your relationship with God, enabling you to live in the fullness of His purpose and provision.

Step 1: Cultivate Daily Time with God

A deeper connection with God begins with consistent, intentional time in His presence. This is where you nurture your relationship with Him through prayer, worship, and the Word.

Scripture:

"But when you pray, go into your room, close the door and pray to your Father, who is unseen. Then your Father, who sees what is done in secret, will reward you." (Matthew 6:6, NIV)

Action Steps:

1. **Set Aside Time Daily:** Dedicate a specific time each day for God, whether in the morning, evening, or another consistent time.

2. **Create a Sacred Space:** Find a quiet place free from distractions to meet with Him.

3. **Use a Journal:** Write down prayers, reflections, and insights from your time with God.

Step 2: Deepen Your Prayer Life

Prayer is a conversation with God that strengthens your relationship with Him. It is both a place of surrender and a means of aligning your heart with His.

Scripture:

"Do not be anxious about anything, but in every situation, by prayer and petition, with thanksgiving, present your requests to God." (Philippians 4:6, NIV)

Action Steps:

1. **Pray with Specificity:** Share your needs, concerns, and desires with God, but also listen for His voice.

2. **Practice Intercessory Prayer:** Pray for others, including family, friends, and the world.

3. **Incorporate Worship and Thanksgiving:** Thank God for His provision and praise Him for who He is.

Prayer Example:

Father, I desire a closer relationship with You. Teach me to pray with sincerity and faith. Help me to hear Your voice and follow Your guidance. In Jesus' name, Amen.

Step 3: Immerse Yourself in God's Word

The Bible is God's voice written for you. Through His Word, you learn His character, promises, and plans for your life.

Scripture:

"Your word is a lamp to my feet and a light to my path." (Psalm 119:105, ESV)

Action Steps:

1. **Read Daily:** Establish a habit of reading the Bible daily, even if it's just a few verses.

2. **Meditate on Scripture:** Reflect on specific verses and ask God how they apply to your life.

3. **Memorize Key Scriptures:** Store God's Word in your heart to draw upon in times of need.

4. **Use Bible Plans:** Follow a reading plan to guide your study and explore topics of interest.

Step 4: Practice Worship and Praise

Worship is more than singing songs—it is an act of surrender, gratitude, and adoration. It brings you into God's presence and helps you focus on His greatness.

Scripture:

"God is spirit, and His worshipers must worship in the Spirit and in truth." (John 4:24, NIV)

Action Steps:

1. **Worship Daily:** Spend time praising God through music, spoken words, or quiet reflection.

2. **Join a Community of Worshippers:** Attend church services or gatherings that foster an atmosphere of worship.

3. **Worship Through Actions:** Let your life reflect your worship by walking in obedience and love.

Step 5: Embrace the Power of the Holy Spirit

The Holy Spirit is your guide, teacher, and helper. By cultivating sensitivity to His leading, you deepen your connection with God and access His power in your life.

Scripture:

"But the Advocate, the Holy Spirit, whom the Father will send in my name, will teach you all things and will remind you of everything I have said to you." (John 14:26, NIV)

Action Steps:

1. **Ask for the Holy Spirit's Guidance:** Pray daily for the Spirit's direction in your decisions.

2. **Listen for His Voice:** Pay attention to the promptings, peace, or conviction He places in your heart.

3. **Walk in the Spirit:** Actively seek to align your thoughts and actions with His leading.

Step 6: Practice Fasting and Spiritual Discipline

Fasting is a spiritual discipline that helps you focus on God and tune out distractions. It strengthens your spirit and enhances your connection with Him.

Scripture:

"But when you fast, anoint your head and wash your face, that your fasting may not be seen by others but by your Father who is

in secret. And your Father who sees in secret will reward you." (Matthew 6:17-18, ESV)

Action Steps:

1. **Choose a Fast:** Decide what to fast from (e.g., food, social media) and for how long.

2. **Set a Purpose:** Fast with a clear intention, such as seeking direction, breaking strongholds, or drawing closer to God.

3. **Combine Fasting with Prayer:** Use the time you would spend on the activity to pray and worship.

Step 7: Seek God Through Community

Connecting with God on a deeper level is enriched by fellowship with other believers. A community provides encouragement, accountability, and shared experiences of God's presence.

Scripture:

"For where two or three gather in My name, there am I with them." (Matthew 18:20, NIV)

Action Steps:

1. **Join a Local Church:** Engage in regular worship, teaching, and fellowship.

2. **Participate in Small Groups:** Join a Bible study or prayer group to grow spiritually with others.

3. **Serve Others:** Use your gifts to contribute to the body of Christ and reflect God's love.

Step 8: Surrender Fully to God

A deeper connection with God requires surrendering every part of your life to Him. Let go of control, and allow Him to lead you in every area, including your finances, relationships, and future.

Scripture:

"Trust in the Lord with all your heart and lean not on your own understanding; in all your ways submit to Him, and He will make your paths straight." (Proverbs 3:5-6, NIV)

Action Steps:

1. **Repent Regularly:** Confess areas where you've fallen short and ask for God's forgiveness.

2. **Offer Your Life as a Sacrifice:** Surrender your plans, desires, and resources to His will.

3. **Trust His Timing:** Wait patiently for God to reveal His plans and provide what you need.

Prayers for Deeper Connection

1. Prayer for Intimacy with God:

Father, I long to know You more. Help me to seek You daily, listen to Your voice, and walk in obedience to Your Word. Draw me closer to Your heart. In Jesus' name, Amen.

2. Prayer for Sensitivity to the Holy Spirit:

Holy Spirit, guide me in all truth and teach me to follow Your leading. Help me to recognize Your voice and trust Your direction. In Jesus' name, Amen.

3. **Prayer of Surrender:**

Lord, I surrender my life to You. Take control of every area—my finances, dreams, and desires. Let Your will be done in me. In Jesus' name, Amen.

Affirmations for Spiritual Growth

- *I hear God's voice clearly and follow His guidance.*

- *The Holy Spirit leads me into truth and empowers me daily.*

- *I am deeply connected to God and walk in His purpose.*

Reflection Questions

1. Are you consistently setting aside time to connect with God?

2. What areas of your life still need to be fully surrendered to Him?

3. How can you deepen your relationship with God through prayer, worship, and the Word?

4. **Living in Divine Connection**

A deep connection with God is the foundation of a fulfilling, purposeful life. When you draw closer to Him, you gain clarity, wisdom, and strength to navigate life's challenges and achieve His plans for you. Prioritize your relationship with God above all else, and you will experience the peace, joy, and freedom that come from living in His presence.

Key Scripture:

"You make known to me the path of life; in Your presence there is fullness of joy; at Your right hand are pleasures forevermore." (Psalm 16:11, ESV)

Chapter 8
Walking in Overflow and Purpose

Living in God's Abundance

God desires His children to live in the overflow of His blessings—not just for their benefit, but to fulfill His purpose and bring glory to His name. Overflow is not limited to material wealth; it encompasses spiritual abundance, joy, peace, relationships, and the ability to impact others through generosity. Walking in overflow means living out your God-given purpose while experiencing the fullness of His provision.

Key Scripture:

"Now to Him who is able to do immeasurably more than all we ask or imagine, according to His power that is at work within us." (Ephesians 3:20, NIV)

This chapter explores how to embrace the abundant life promised by God and align it with your divine purpose.

Step 1: Understand Overflow from God's Perspective

Scripture:

"The thief comes only to steal and kill and destroy; I have come that they may have life, and have it to the full." (John 10:10, NIV)

Overflow is not about accumulating wealth for selfish gain but stewarding God's blessings in a way that reflects His heart. It is about living in divine provision while advancing the Kingdom of God.

Key Principles of Godly Overflow:

1. **It Begins with the Heart:** God looks at your heart and motives. True overflow comes to those who prioritize Him over material things.

2. **It Flows from Obedience:** Walking in God's overflow requires aligning with His principles in every area of your life.

3. **It Has a Kingdom Purpose:** God blesses you so you can be a blessing to others (Genesis 12:2).

Step 2: Walk in Your God-Given Purpose

Scripture:

"For we are God's handiwork, created in Christ Jesus to do good works, which God prepared in advance for us to do." (Ephesians 2:10, NIV)

God has a unique purpose for your life. Fulfilling that purpose is the key to experiencing true overflow. When you walk in alignment with His plan, you discover the joy of using your gifts and resources for His glory.

Action Steps:

1. **Discover Your Purpose:** Seek God in prayer and reflection to understand your calling. What are your passions, talents, and spiritual gifts?

2. **Align Your Goals with His Plan:** Ensure your financial, personal, and spiritual goals support your divine purpose.

3. **Serve Others:** Purpose is often found in service. Look for ways to use your resources and abilities to meet the needs of others.

Step 3: Develop a Mindset of Abundance

Scripture:

"And God is able to bless you abundantly, so that in all things at all times, having all that you need, you will abound in every good work." (2 Corinthians 9:8, NIV)

Walking in overflow begins in your mind. An abundant mindset sees God as the source of all provision and trusts Him to meet every need.

Action Steps:

1. **Reject the Scarcity Mentality:** Do not let fear or doubt limit your faith in God's ability to provide.

2. **Speak Words of Faith:** Declare God's promises over your life and finances.

3. **Focus on God's Faithfulness:** Reflect on past instances where God has provided abundantly.

Affirmation:

I live in the abundance of God's provision, and I trust Him to meet all my needs according to His riches in glory.

Step 4: Steward Your Resources Wisely

Scripture:

"Whoever can be trusted with very little can also be trusted with much." (Luke 16:10, NIV)

God's blessings come with responsibility. Stewardship involves managing your time, talents, and treasures in a way that honors Him and advances His Kingdom.

Action Steps:

1. **Give Generously:** Tithe faithfully, give offerings, and support those in need.

2. **Plan Your Spending:** Use a budget to manage your finances wisely and avoid wastefulness.

3. **Invest in Eternal Rewards:** Use your resources to support ministries, missions, and Kingdom work.

Step 5: Live Generously

Scripture:

"Give, and it will be given to you. A good measure, pressed down, shaken together and running over, will be poured into your lap." (Luke 6:38, NIV)

Generosity is both a fruit of living in overflow and a key to maintaining it. When you give freely, you open the door for God to pour even more blessings into your life.

Action Steps:

1. **Give With Joy:** Let your giving be an act of worship, not obligation.

2. **Bless Others in Secret:** Give without seeking recognition, trusting that God sees your heart.

3. **Be Open-Handed:** Be willing to share your time, resources, and wisdom with those in need.

Step 6: Trust God for Continuous Provision

Scripture:

"And my God will meet all your needs according to the riches of His glory in Christ Jesus." (Philippians 4:19, NIV)

Walking in overflow requires continual reliance on God as your provider. Trusting Him allows you to live in peace, knowing He will meet every need.

Action Steps:

1. **Practice Gratitude:** Regularly thank God for His provision and blessings.

2. **Surrender Your Plans:** Allow God to guide your financial decisions and trust His timing.

3. **Rest in His Promises:** Meditate on scriptures that affirm God's provision and faithfulness.

Step 7: Impact the Kingdom with Your Overflow

Scripture:

"You will be enriched in every way so that you can be generous on every occasion, and through us your generosity will result in thanksgiving to God." (2 Corinthians 9:11, NIV)

Overflow is not meant to stop with you; it is designed to flow through you. When you use your abundance to bless others and advance God's work, you multiply its impact for eternity.

Action Steps:

1. **Support Ministries and Missions:** Use your resources to spread the gospel and support those in need.

2. **Mentor Others:** Teach others how to walk in financial freedom and live out their purpose.

3. **Leave a Legacy:** Plan for future generations by creating a financial and spiritual inheritance.

Prayers for Overflow and Purpose

1. Prayer for Abundance:

Father, I thank You for Your overflowing blessings in my life. Help me to steward them wisely and use them to fulfill Your purpose. In Jesus' name, Amen.

2. Prayer for Purpose:

Lord, reveal Your plan for my life. Guide me to walk in my calling and use my gifts to glorify You. In Jesus' name, Amen.

3. Prayer for Generosity:

God, create in me a generous heart. Teach me to give freely and trust You as my source. Let my life be a reflection of Your love and provision. In Jesus' name, Amen.

Affirmations for Overflow and Purpose

- *I live in the overflow of God's blessings and walk in His purpose for my life.*

- *God provides all I need, and I trust Him as my source.*

- *I am a faithful steward of God's resources and a blessing to others.*

Reflection Questions

1. How do you define overflow in your life?

2. Are you using your resources to fulfill God's purpose?

3. What steps can you take to steward your blessings and live generously?

A Life of Overflow and Purpose

Walking in overflow and purpose is about aligning your life with God's will, trusting Him as your source, and using His blessings to impact others. It is a journey of faith, stewardship, and Kingdom-minded living. When you embrace God's abundance and walk in your divine calling, you become a vessel through which His blessings flow to the world.

Key Scripture:

"The Lord will open the heavens, the storehouse of His bounty, to send rain on your land in season and to bless all the work of your hands. You will lend to many nations but will borrow from none." (Deuteronomy 28:12, NIV)

Conclusion

Financial Freedom

As we come to the end of this journey, I want to remind you that financial freedom is not just a destination—it is a way of living that aligns with God's will and purpose for your life. Throughout this book, we have explored the principles of wealth and success from a biblical perspective, and we've seen how God desires His children to walk in abundance, not for selfish gain, but for the advancement of His Kingdom.

True financial freedom begins when we understand that our identity in Christ is one of royalty and inheritance. As co-heirs with Christ (Romans 8:17), we have been given access to the resources of heaven and the wisdom needed to manage them effectively. It is only through Him that we can experience true overflow—not just in our finances but in our relationships, health, and spiritual growth.

The path to financial success is built on faith, stewardship, and purpose. It requires a deep trust in God's provision, a commitment to managing resources wisely, and a heart that desires to bless others. By applying biblical principles—such as tithing, generosity, wise investing, and budgeting—you are positioning yourself to live in the fullness of God's promises. Remember, the overflow is not just for you; it is meant to bless others and bring glory to God.

As you continue this journey toward financial freedom, keep these truths in mind:

- **God is your ultimate provider.** Trust Him to meet all your needs (Philippians 4:19).

- **You are called to steward what He has entrusted to you.** Be diligent, disciplined, and wise (Proverbs 21:5).

- **You are a blessing to others.** Generosity is a reflection of your heart for God and others (Luke 6:38).

- **Your purpose is bigger than finances.** Let your financial journey be a tool to fulfill the calling God has placed on your life (Ephesians 2:10).

I encourage you to take the steps outlined in this book seriously. Whether it's setting financial goals, creating a budget, paying off debt, or giving generously, each step will bring you closer to experiencing the freedom and purpose that God has designed for you. Trust in His timing, seek His guidance, and watch how He will use your obedience to bring about breakthrough and overflow in your life.

Prayer for Your Journey:

Father, I thank You for the wisdom and understanding You have provided throughout this book. I commit to living in alignment with Your financial principles, trusting You as my provider and guide. Help me to be faithful in managing the resources You've entrusted to me. I surrender my finances, my goals, and my plans into Your hands, knowing that You will direct my path. May my life be a reflection of Your abundance and glory. In Yeshua's name, Amen.

As you continue to walk in the power and abundance that comes from knowing Christ, remember that you are destined for more than just financial freedom—you are destined for a life of purpose, impact, and eternal reward. Let God lead you into the overflow, and may you live out His plan for your life with joy, peace, and confidence in His provision.

Key Scripture to Reflect Upon:

"But seek first His kingdom and His righteousness, and all these things will be given to you as well." (Matthew 6:33, NIV)

May you experience the fullness of God's promises as you walk in financial freedom, purpose, and divine overflow.

Appendices

PRACTICAL TOOLS FOR FINANCIAL FREEDOM AND SUCCESS IN GOD

The appendices of this book provide additional resources, tools, and reflections to help you apply the principles and insights shared throughout. These resources are designed to help you stay on track as you pursue financial freedom, walk in overflow, and live out your divine purpose.

Appendix A: Biblical Financial Principles Cheat Sheet

This cheat sheet summarizes key biblical financial principles that align with God's plan for your financial freedom. Keep this handy for daily reflection and guidance.

1. **God is Your Provider**

Scripture: "The Lord is my shepherd; I shall not want." (Psalm 23:1)

Trust that God is your ultimate source of provision, and do not rely on your own understanding.

2. **Stewardship**

Scripture: "It is required of stewards that they be found trustworthy." (1 Corinthians 4:2)

God calls us to manage the resources He gives us wisely, knowing that everything belongs to Him.

3. **Generosity and Giving**

Scripture: "Give, and it will be given to you." (Luke 6:38)

The principle of sowing and reaping—when you give generously, God promises to bless you abundantly.

4. Avoiding Debt

Scripture: "The borrower is slave to the lender." (Proverbs 22:7)

Strive to live free from debt and use your finances to serve God's purposes, not to be enslaved by financial obligations.

5. Planning and Budgeting

Scripture: "The plans of the diligent lead surely to abundance, but everyone who is hasty comes only to poverty." (Proverbs 21:5)

God values wise planning and budgeting. Create a financial plan that honors Him and helps you achieve your goals.

Appendix B: Scriptures for Financial Success and Freedom

This section offers a compilation of powerful Scriptures that can encourage and strengthen your faith on your financial journey.

1. Provision and Abundance

"And God is able to bless you abundantly, so that in all things at all times, having all that you need, you will abound in every good work." (2 Corinthians 9:8)

"The Lord will open the heavens, the storehouse of His bounty, to send rain on your land in season and to bless all the work of your hands." (Deuteronomy 28:12)

2. Wisdom in Financial Decisions

"If any of you lacks wisdom, let him ask of God, who gives to all liberally and without reproach, and it will be given to him." (James 1:5)

"For wisdom will enter your heart, and knowledge will be pleasant to your soul." (Proverbs 2:10)

3. Debt and Prosperity

"The rich rule over the poor, and the borrower is slave to the lender." (Proverbs 22:7)

"You will lend to many nations but will borrow from none." (Deuteronomy 28:12)

4. Generosity and Giving

"Give, and it will be given to you. A good measure, pressed down, shaken together and running over, will be poured into your lap." (Luke 6:38)

"Each of you should give what you have decided in your heart to give, not reluctantly or under compulsion, for God loves a cheerful giver." (2 Corinthians 9:7)

Appendix C: Practical Budgeting Tools and Financial Planning Worksheets

This section includes tools and worksheets designed to help you apply biblical financial principles practically. These resources are intended to guide you in budgeting, debt reduction, and planning for your future.

1. Monthly Budget Worksheet

A simple monthly budget helps you track income, expenses, and savings. Create a worksheet that:

- List all sources of income.

- Track fixed and variable expenses (rent, utilities, groceries, etc.).

- Set aside amounts for savings, tithing, and giving.

- Adjust as necessary to maintain a balanced budget.

2. Debt Repayment Plan

If you are working to get out of debt, create a worksheet that:

- List all outstanding debts, including credit cards, loans, and any other obligations.

- Prioritize debts by interest rate or amount.

- Set up a plan to pay off the smallest debts first (the "snowball" method) or target high-interest debts (the "avalanche" method).

3. Savings and Investment Plan

This worksheet template helps you:

- Identify short- and long-term savings goals (emergency fund, retirement, etc.).

- Set specific target amounts and deadlines for each goal.

- Research and decide on investment options that align with your faith and financial goals.

4. Giving Tracker

Create a "giving tracker" which allows you to monitor your charitable contributions and track your generosity. Use it to:

- Record tithes and offerings.

- Set goals for increasing your giving over time.

- Reflect on how your giving impacts your financial health and spiritual growth.

Appendix D: Affirmations for Financial Success and Purpose

This section provides a list of daily affirmations that align your mindset with God's principles of financial freedom and purpose. Recite these affirmations regularly to strengthen your faith and beliefs about wealth, abundance, and your identity in Christ.

1. *I am a child of God, and I am called to live in His abundance.*

2. *God is my provider, and I trust Him to meet all my needs according to His riches in glory.*

3. *I walk in financial freedom, debt-free, and with wisdom in managing my resources.*

4. *I am generous and cheerful in my giving, knowing that God will bless me abundantly.*

5. *I am walking in my divine purpose, and all that I do is for God's glory.*

6. *I have been given the wisdom, knowledge, and understanding to make sound financial decisions.*

Appendix E: Recommended Resources for Further Study

This section lists additional books and websites that can help you grow in your understanding of financial freedom from a biblical perspective.

1. **Other Books:**

   "The Blessed Life" by Robert Morris

   "Financial Freedom" by Hezekiah L. Walker

   "The Total Money Makeover" by Dave Ramsey

2. **Websites:**

Dave Ramsey: www.daveramsey.com

Crown Financial Ministries: www.crown.org

Kingdom Advisors: www.kingdomadvisors.com

Appendix F: Prayer for Financial Breakthrough and Overflow

Prayer for Breakthrough:

Father, I thank You for Your faithfulness and provision in my life. I repent for any areas where I've not honored You with my finances. I surrender my money, resources, and plans into Your hands. Lord, open the doors of financial breakthrough in my life. Release Your overflow into my finances and guide me with wisdom as I steward the resources You've entrusted to me. Help me to walk in financial freedom and in alignment with Your will. In Yeshua's name, Amen.

Prayer for Overflow and Purpose:

Lord, thank You for calling me to live in abundance and overflow. I recognize that all that I have is from You, and I commit to using my resources to fulfill Your purpose. Help me to walk in Your will, trusting that You will meet my needs and enable me to be a blessing to others. May my life and finances reflect Your Kingdom. In Yeshua's name, Amen.

As you embark on the journey to financial freedom, remember that it is a process. Trust that God is working in your life, and keep your eyes fixed on Him. Stay faithful to the principles you've learned, remain persistent in your efforts, and always rely on the Holy Spirit to guide your decisions. With God's help, you can walk in the fullness of His abundance, fulfilling your purpose and impacting others for His Kingdom.

Key Scripture:

"Commit to the Lord whatever you do, and He will establish your plans." (Proverbs 16:3, NIV)

May you experience His provision, peace, and prosperity as you walk in financial freedom and purpose.